Invitations to Personal Reading
Curriculum Foundation Classroom Library
Scott, Foresman and Company

Realistic Stories	
Betsy's Little Star	Carolyn Haywood
Emmett's Pig	Mary Stolz
Mop Top	Don Freeman
Nobody Listens to Andrew	Elizabeth Guilfoile
A Pair of Red Clogs	Masako Matsuno
Animals —True and Imaginary	
Baby Elephant's Trunk	Sesyle Joslin
Little Black Puppy	Charlotte Zolotow
The No-Bark Dog	Stan Williamson
Seven Diving Ducks	Margaret Friskey
The Unhappy Hippopotamus	Nancy Moore
Fun and Fancy	
Four Fur Feet	Margaret Wise Brown
Georgie to the Rescue	Robert Bright
The Mitten	retold by Alvin Tresselt
No Fighting, No Biting!	Else Minarik
The Three Wishes	retold by Joseph Jacobs
Books to Enrich the Content Fields	
The Big Book of Real Building and Wrecking Machines	George Zaffo
Columbus	Ingri and Edgar d'Aulaire
Space Alphabet	Irene Zacks
What Is A Frog	Gene Darby
What's Inside?	May Garelick
Books Too Good to Miss	
Away We Go!	compiled by Catherine McEwen
Hide and Seek Fog	Alvin Tresselt
I Wish, I Wish	Lisl Weil
Inch by Inch	Leo Lionni
Otto in Africa	William Pène du Bois

What's Inside?

By May Garelick

Photographs By Rena Jakobsen

THE STORY OF AN EGG THAT HATCHED

New York: William R. Scott, Inc., Publisher

Special Scott, Foresman and Company Edition
for the *Invitations to Personal Reading* Program

PRINTED IN THE U.S.A.

Library of Congress Cat. Card No. 55-5099

TEXT COPYRIGHT MCMLV BY MAY GARELICK. PHOTOGRAPHS COPYRIGHT MCMLV BY RENA JAKOBSEN.

Photograph Processing by John Albert

This edition is printed and distributed by Scott, Foresman and Company by special arrangement with
William R. Scott, Inc., New York, N. Y.

WHAT'S INSIDE?

WHAT'S INSIDE?

Written by MAY GARELICK
Illustrated with Photographs by RENA JACOBSEN

This is a very simple nature story about how an egg is hatched, crack by crack, all in photographs. The easy-to-read text keeps children guessing about what will come out of the egg and what life will begin.

* * *

Dewey Decimal Classification: E

Here is an egg—a big white egg.

See the shell of the egg?
There's a crack in it.

See the crack?

Now the crack is bigger.

What can be breaking the egg
and making it crack?

Sssh! Sssh!
There's a little noise
coming from inside the egg.
A little tapping noise—
tap, tap, tap.

What is going on inside this egg, anyway?

Now look.
The crack is so big you can see
something starting to push through.

What can it be?
A head?
A beak?

What is pushing through the shell?
Can it be a horse?
A hippopotamus?
A kangaroo?

Oh no! Whoever heard of a hippopotamus
hatching out of an egg?
And whoever saw a horse with a beak?

Ooh! *Now* look what's happening.

Feathers—look at all the feathers.

First a beak and then feathers—
and *now* something that looks like
feet.

What *has* feathers, feet, and a beak
and comes out of an egg?

A chicken?

It might be.
A chicken comes out of an egg.

But a chicken's egg is smaller than our egg.
So, it can't be a chicken.

Can it be a robin?

No.
Robins' eggs are much smaller.
And besides, they are blue.
It's not a robin.

Then what kind of bird is it?

Is it a turkey?

Turkeys are birds, too.
Turkeys hatch from eggs.

But our egg is bigger than a turkey's egg.
It can't be a turkey.

Can it be an ostrich?
Oh, no!

An ostrich comes from a *huge* egg.

Whatever kind of a bird he is,
he has worked hard to come out
of his shell and be born.

He is tired, and sleepy, and wet.
He has to rest and dry his feathers.

Now his feathers are drying out,
and he is not so tired.

Now, can you tell what kind of a bird he is?

Look at his feet—they are webbed.
Why would a bird have webbed feet?

Webbed feet to paddle the water.
Webbed feet for swimming.
What bird swims?

Did you say "duck"?

Anybody might think it's a duck, but it isn't.
It's a goose—a little baby goose.
A baby gosling.
Cheep, cheep, cheep.

And it has taken this gosling
a whole day and a whole night
to break through the shell and be born.

But a goose isn't born in a day.
Lots of things happened before this day.

Thirty days before the little gosling was born the mother goose built a nest.

Sometimes the father goose helped her, but mostly she built the nest herself with damp straw that she gathered from around the farmyard.

When the nest was finished, she plucked some feathers from her breast and spread the soft, soft feathers on top of the straw.

Then, in the warm, soft nest she could lay her eggs.

Sometimes she laid lots of eggs, but this time there were only two.

Day after day, and night after night, she sat on the eggs.

But the eggs wouldn't hatch unless they were warmed *all* over—so, with her beak and with her webbed feet she turned the eggs and sat on them some more.

The father goose, the gander, never sat on the eggs. But he was always close by to protect them and to be with the mother. He watched the nest, and if a stranger came near, the gander would flap his big wings, let out a loud honk and a hiss, and chase the stranger away.

Once in a while the mother goose had to leave the nest to get something to eat. But before she did, she always covered the eggs over with some straw to protect them and keep them warm.

Then she could go to look for food, and take a drink, and a quick swim in the pond.

But she never stayed away long. After her swim she would come right back to the nest and wet the eggs with her wet feathers.

She had to wet them. The eggs wouldn't hatch unless she did.

For a whole month she did these same things every day.

Every day she sat on the eggs.

Once each day, she turned them.

After each swim, she wet them.

All this she did to help her babies—to make it easier for them to break through the shell and get born.

Then, one day, from inside one of the shells, she hears a little tapping noise—*tap, tap, tap.*

The mother goose knows that at last one of her babies is stirring inside the egg.

At last the baby is ready to come out of the shell. Now there is nothing more the mother goose can do for him. The gosling must break through the shell by himself. She cannot help him.

The shell is tough and strong to protect him, so it is hard for the weak, little gosling to break it. With a tiny sharp point near the end of his beak he hammers at the shell. Little by little he breaks away enough of the shell so his beak can come out. Now he can breathe the fresh air.

All the long day and night the weak little bird works and rests. He works to break through the shell and hatch out.

Finally, after a day and a night of hammering and resting, the little gosling is all out of the shell.

A baby goose is born!

In all this time the mother goose was close to the nest waiting for her babies to hatch.

First one baby hatched. And now, soon, her second baby will hatch out of his shell.

Now the mother goose can help her babies again.

When they first come out of their wet shells, the baby goslings are all wet. So, the mother goose snuggles her wet, tired babies close to her to dry them off with her feathers and with the warmth from her body.

After a few hours, when the baby goslings are dry, one of them tries to stand up. At first his legs are shaky, but he keeps trying and trying, until finally, he can stand up all right.

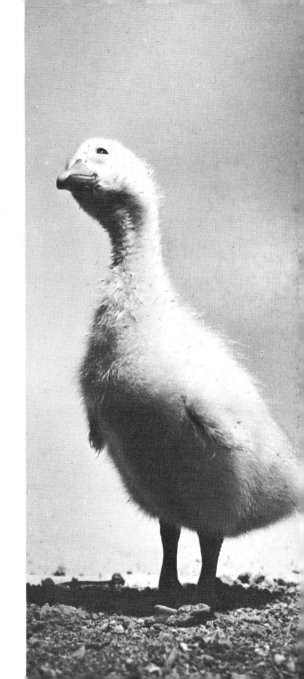

When the babies are stronger,
the mother goose walks away from the nest,
and her two little goslings follow her.

The father goose joins them.
The family takes a short walk.

The mother goose finds some soft green grass.
She picks at it with her beak,
but she doesn't eat the grass.
She is just showing her babies how to eat.

One baby gosling does what his mother does.
He picks at the grass.

The grass tastes good to the little gosling.
He eats it.
He is so busy eating that he wanders away
from his family.

He is *so* busy eating that he does not see
the big cat sitting very still on top of the rock.

The baby gosling never saw a cat before.
He doesn't know that baby birds
must stay away from cats.

But the father goose sees the cat
and sets up a loud quuuuck, *quuuuck,*
quuuuuuck. He frightens the cat,
and the scared cat runs away.

Now the baby gosling is back—
safe with his family.

After a while the mother goose leads her goslings
into the water.
Geese are water birds and they like to swim.
The little goslings aren't afraid of the water.
They walk right in and swim away.

Every day the little baby goslings will swim.
They will eat and sleep and grow.
They will grow into big, white, fluffy geese
just like their parents.

Is this the end of the story?
No—when the baby goslings grow up
they will have babies of their own
that will hatch out of eggs
just as they did.

This story never ends.
It goes on and on and on.